NIGERIA

GROLIER EDUCATIONAL
SHERMAN TURNPIKE, DANBURY, CONNECTICUT 06816

GC PM

Published 1997 by Grolier Educational
Sherman Turnpike, Danbury, Connecticut.
Copyright © 1997 Marshall Cavendish Limited.

Set ISBN : 0-7172-9099-9
Volume ISBN : 0-7172-9103-0

Library of Congress Cataloging-in-Publication Data
Nigeria
p.cm. -- (Fiesta!)
Includes index.
Summary: Describes the customs and beliefs connected to some of the special occasions celebrated in Nigeria, including the Mmanwe Festival, Osun Ceremony, Independence Day, and others.
Includes recipes and related activities.
ISBN 0-7172-9103-0
1. Festivals -- Nigeria -- Juvenile literature. 2. Nigeria -- Social life and customs -- Juvenile literature.
[1. Festivals -- Nigeria. 2. Holidays -- Nigeria. 3. Nigeria -- Social life and customs.]
I. Grolier Educational (Firm) II. Series: Fiesta! (Danbury, Conn.)
GT4889.N6N55   1997
394.269669--dc21
97-18671
CIP
AC

Marshall Cavendish Limited
Editorial staff
Editorial Director: Ellen Dupont
Series Designer: Joyce Mason
Crafts devised and created by Susan Moxley
Music arrangements by Harry Boteler
Photographs by Bruce Mackie
Subeditors: Susan Janes, Judy Fovargue
Production: Craig Chubb

Author

For this volume
Editor: Tessa Paul
Writer: Tim Cooke
Designer: Trevor Vertigan
Editorial Assistant: Lorien Kite
Consultant: Anthony Adeloye,
Chief Librarian, Nigerian High Commission, London

Printed in Italy

Adult supervision advised for all crafts and recipes
particularly those involving sharp instruments and heat.

CONTENTS

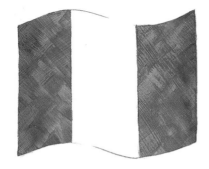

NIGERIA:

More people live in Nigeria than in any other country in Africa. Oilfields, mines, and forests make it one of the richest countries on the continent.

▼ Two great religions,
Christianity and Islam, live side by side. A minority of Nigerians follow traditional beliefs.

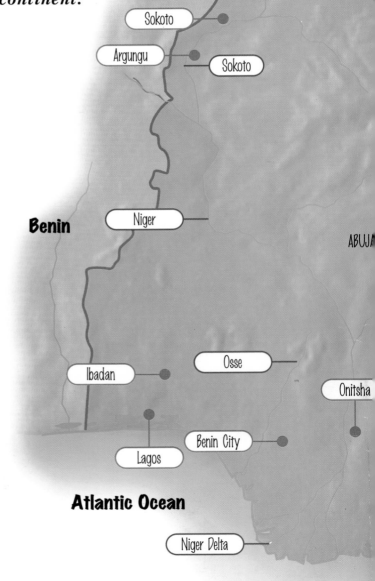

Sokoto

Argungu

Sokoto

Benin

Niger

ABUJA

Osse

Ibadan

Onitsha

Benin City

Lagos

Atlantic Ocean

Niger Delta

4

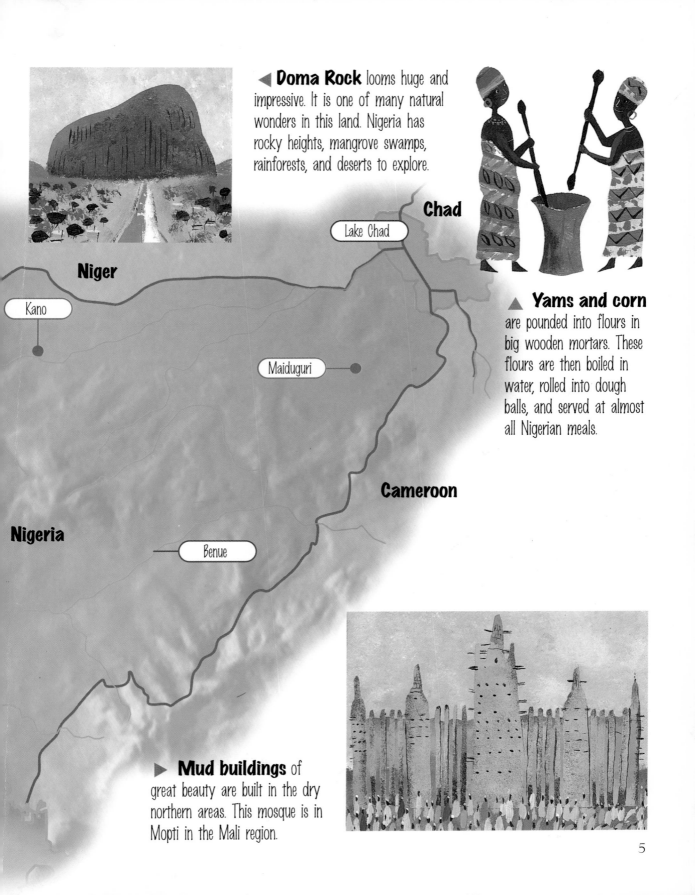

Doma Rock looms huge and impressive. It is one of many natural wonders in this land. Nigeria has rocky heights, mangrove swamps, rainforests, and deserts to explore.

Chad

Lake Chad

Niger

Kano

Maiduguri

Yams and corn are pounded into flours in big wooden mortars. These flours are then boiled in water, rolled into dough balls, and served at almost all Nigerian meals.

Cameroon

Nigeria

Benue

Mud buildings of great beauty are built in the dry northern areas. This mosque is in Mopti in the Mali region.

RELIGIONS

There are three main religions in Nigeria. Islam and Christianity are both popular, and many people also remain faithful to parts of the ancient tribal beliefs.

NIGERIA has more people than any African country. Almost half of the country's population are Muslims. They follow the Islamic faith. About a third of the people are Christians. Some are Catholics, and others are Protestants. Only one in five Nigerians still follows the traditional beliefs, but Protestant churches often mix these old beliefs with Christianity.

ISLAM is the name of the faith followed by Muslims. They believe in one supreme god called Allah. Islam was begun in the 7th century by the prophet Mohammed.

This elaborate metal cross shows how Nigerians have adapted traditional art to the symbols of Christianity.

It began in Arabia and soon spread to north Africa. Through the Arab slave trade in Africa the faith took hold in west and east Africa, including Nigeria. Its laws are contained in a holy book called the Koran. Nigerians, like other Muslims, must pray five times a day. Their main festival is Ramadan, when for 30 days they cannot eat or drink during the hours of daylight. Nigerian Muslims live mainly in the north of the country. Their leader is called the Sultan of Sokoto.

CHRISTIANITY first came to Nigeria from Europe in the 16th century. The most important Christian festivals are Christmas and Easter.

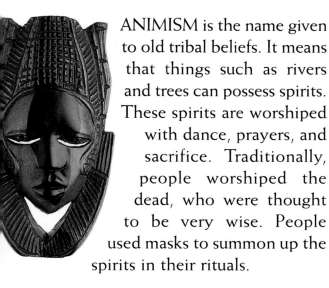

ANIMISM is the name given to old tribal beliefs. It means that things such as rivers and trees can possess spirits. These spirits are worshiped with dance, prayers, and sacrifice. Traditionally, people worshiped the dead, who were thought to be very wise. People used masks to summon up the spirits in their rituals.

FOLK SONGS

There are no Nigerian folk songs in this book. Nigerian folk songs are not written down like other songs. Instead the tunes and words vary according to the occasion. They are different every time. Because there are no songs in this book does not mean that music is not important. All over Nigeria you can hear drums, singing, and traditional instruments.

GREETINGS FROM **NIGERIA!**

Nigeria's population of some 95 million people belongs to more than 250 different groups. The biggest are the Hausa people of the north, the Yoruba of the southwest, and the Ibo of the southeast. Together they make up over half the population.

English is the official language, which comes from the days when Great Britain ruled Nigeria. But most people also speak

Hausa, Yoruba, or Ibo, depending on where they live. The greetings translated here are in Yoruba. In southern Nigeria many people speak pidgin English. This began as a kind of simple English but has now developed into a complex language of its own.

How do you say...

Hello

She alaafia ni

Goodbye

O daabo

Thank you

E shee

Peace

Ohilaja

LEBOKU

The Yakurr people of southern Nigeria celebrate the harvest with a whole week of traditional rituals and dancing.

In August each year the Yakurr people celebrate *Leboku*, the festival that marks the yam harvest. Yams are roots, a little like sweet potatoes. They are the Yakurr's main crop, so a good harvest is a reason to celebrate.

Leboku lasts seven days. The Yakurr hold feasts and rituals. But the real heart of the celebration is dancing to furious drumming. It is a noisy affair. The drummers begin playing as early as 4 a.m.

There are two main dances. *Ekoi* is for men, and *Ekeledei* is for women. The Ekoi is the Yakurr's chief. Drummers use "talking" drums, which sound like an African language, to call the Ekoi and the high priests to the dance. They all wear costumes, and their feet are painted. They wave small brushes. Two men dance the Ekoi. They have sheep fleece on their arms and wave swords. The dance is based on ancient movements for fighting.

Ekeledei girls wear brass leg rings up to their knees and cloth ankle bands. They adorn their hair with fine peacock feathers. They decide the order to stand in during the dance by holding a wrestling tournament.

Another big part of Leboku is called *Yekpi*, which is similar to April Fool's Day.

Young men perform feats of strength that they say are done by magic. People pretend to be rude to each other. On this day everybody has fun.

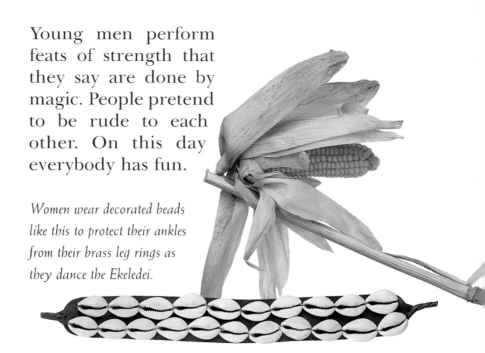

Women wear decorated beads like this to protect their ankles from their brass leg rings as they dance the Ekeledei.

This instrument is made from a hollow gourd and is decorated with elaborate carving. Small brushes of horse hair like this one are waved during the dance to brush away evil spirits. They also keep away the flies.

YAM FUFU

SERVES 4 TO 6
2 pounds white-fleshed yams
Salt (optional)
Banana leaves, to serve
(optional)

1 Using a vegetable peeler, peel yams. Cut into chunks.
2 Bring a large pan of water to a boil over high heat. Add yam chunks, and return water to a boil. Boil until yam chunks are very tender when pierced with tip of a knife.
3 Drain the yams in a colander, in the sink.

4 Using a pestle and mortar, or a potato masher, mash the yams until smooth, like mashed potatoes. Add salt if you prefer.
5 Spoon onto banana leaves or into a bowl to serve. This is traditionally served with stews.

THE MAGIC DRUM

It is hard work tilling the land to grow food to feed your family.

Often the weather turns bad, and the crops fail. This is a story

about the great importance of work and the harvest.

ONCE UPON A TIME there lived a very wise king. Nobody in his kingdom ever went hungry, even when the harvest failed. The king had a magic drum, and whenever the harvest was poor, he drummed on it. Vast amounts of food would appear, spread out on tables ready to eat. Then the king held huge feasts, to which he invited everyone for miles around, and even some of the local animals. The only thing that the king was not generous with was his drum. He guarded it carefully, as it was the source of food for his people.

Tortoise, the laziest animal in the forest, was plotting to take the drum away and keep the food for himself and his own family. He did not think of other people's hunger in time of famine.

One day the queen and her daughter were taking a walk when a coconut fell and broke open in front of them. High up on a rock, Tortoise waited. "What good luck," thought the queen and gave it to her daughter to eat. As soon as the little girl had finished the fruit, Tortoise rolled down from the high rock where he was spying.

He shouted, "Give me back my coconut." The queen simply smiled.

When they all got back to the village, Tortoise told the king that he, Tortoise, had worked very hard for the coconut that had been taken from him.

"I will repay you," said the king. "You can have anything that you want."

Immediately Tortoise replied, "I'll have your magic drum." The queen was

amazed when the king agreed and gave it to Tortoise. The king did not tell Tortoise that if its owner were ever to walk over a stick in his path, the drum refused to make food. Instead, when it was used, three hundred angry warriors would appear and beat the drummer. The king knew that Tortoise was bound to step over a stick as he plodded along.

Sure enough, Tortoise came back the next day, covered in dents. "I have come to return your drum," he said. "Instead of a feast I got a beating." "Thank you, Tortoise," stated the king, "This drum is like the land; in the right hands it yields a good harvest. If you are mean and lazy, you and your family will always go hungry."

FISHING FESTIVAL

For more than 400 years the end of the fishing season has been marked by a festival at Argungu, on the Rima River in the northwest of Nigeria.

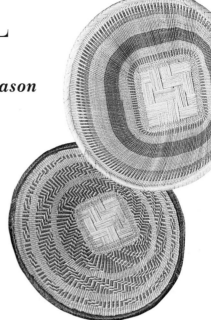

The date of the festival changes from year to year. It usually takes place on a Saturday in February or early in March. The precise day is set by the Emir of Argungu, the local ruler. He is also the guest of honor at the festival.

Nigeria has a great many rivers, and fish are therefore a very important food. This famous fishing festival began in the 16th century, to mark the end of the fishing season.

The festival takes place at a pavilion built beside the river. The events include archery, wrestling, and boxing, as well as music and dancing.

The main event is a fishing competition. Hundreds of men form a line a mile long about a quarter of a

This statuette shows the Emir of Argungu being protected from the sun by a parasol. The decorated fabric is designed to celebrate the festival.

mile from the river. Each carries a large hollow gourd and two nets, which look like the wings of a huge butterfly. This is the traditional way of fishing in Nigeria.

With a sign from the Emir a gun is fired. The fishermen charge forward into the river, which becomes a seething mass of men and nets. After two hours another shot signals the end of the competition. Whoever catches the largest fish gets a prize. The season is over on the river for another year.

Nigerians preserve fish by drying them in salt. Before refrigeration this was the main way of preserving fish all over the world. The fish tastes strong and salty.

FISH STEW

SERVES 6

¼ cup finely chopped parsley
1 onion, finely chopped
½ red bell pepper, finely chopped
2¼ pounds fish fillets, skinned
⅓ cup peanut oil
3 tbsp tomato paste
½ cup fish stock or water
½ cup each sliced red and green bell peppers
1½ cups diced potatoes

1 Combine parsley, onions, and chopped pepper in a bowl.
2 Place some of the parsley mixture on top of one fillet. Roll over. Secure with a tooth pick. Repeat with remaining fillets.
3 Heat oil in Dutch oven. Add fish and fry until brown. Stir in tomato paste, stock, and diced potatoes. Add any left-over parsley mixture and sliced peppers. Cover.
4 Simmer 20 minutes, until potatoes are cooked. Serve the stew with rice.

MMANWE FESTIVAL

This annual festival celebrates tribal tradition. Craftsmen display their masks and perform to the beat of "talking" drums.

Masks no longer play as significant a role in Nigerian life as they once did. But they still feature in spectacular ceremonies held each December in the south of the country, where a very important festival is held in the province of Anambra.

Many masks are based on the animals of the bush. Tribal people usually live quite near wild creatures, and they naturally borrow designs from, say, the spots of a leopard or a zebra's stripes.

Among these people there are

By holding the strings of this drum, drummers make it sound as if it is talking the Yoruba language.

secret societies that choose certain animals as their "totems" or emblems. They hope that if they resemble that animal, they will become as fierce or brave as it is.

Nigerians used to believe that masks

Elaborate masks help the people who wear them take on a different character, which might be that of an ancestor or of a particular animal, such as a giraffe.

Today's festivals are held to preserve the old mask-making traditions, despite the fact that the beliefs behind the masks are no longer remembered or are not important.

A festival highlight is the display of rare masks. The most powerful of all is known as *Ijele*, which means king of masks.

allowed people to take on the character of their ancestors, whom they used to worship. By wearing masks, people thought that they could be as wise as their respected ancestors.

MAKE YOUR OWN MASK

African masks were carved and decorated with bones, claws, and teeth. Make your own, but pattern it with raffia, buttons, and feathers.

The masks of Africa used to play an important role in tribal life. The magic men of medicine wore them; the priests and judges hid behind them. Masks covered the ordinary human face and brought special qualities to the wearer. The people who were not in masks felt the power of the mask and would do whatever the masked one told them to do. Masks often resembled animals. Certain qualities of the animal were exaggerated. A leopard-mask may be given a huge row of sharp teeth, or the pale, sharp eyes of a lion would become big and scary on the mask. Masks were made to frighten. The masked one could pick out a wrongdoer or a criminal. The mask would scare the guilty person into a confession.

Masks are now works of art, showing the skill of the craftsman. Make one to put on the wall or wear to a party.

YOU WILL NEED
A balloon
Newspaper and cardboard
Wallpaper paste
Poster paints
Raffia
Feathers

1 Blow up a balloon to the size and shape of your head. Cover the balloon with long strips of newspaper, painted with wallpaper paste. Tie a string to the knot of the balloon, and hang it up to dry. Draw a clear line around the papier-mâché sphere, and then cut it in half with a pair of scissors. Discard one of the halves, or use it make a second mask. You now have your basic mask shape.

2 Cover the cut edges of the half-sphere with small scraps of newspaper and wallpaper paste. Make the eyebrows, nose, mouth, and whiskers with pieces of twisted newspaper that have been covered with paste. Allow them to dry, then stick on the cardboard teeth. Paint the mask white, then leave it to dry once more.

3 Decorate the mask with poster paints. Once the paint has dried, poke a hole in the center of each eye, to see through. Then poke four holes along the edge of mask near the whiskers. Thread the strips of raffia through these holes. Finally stick some feathers into the top of the mask.

17

REGATTA

Every year Nigerians celebrate the role rivers play in their lives with festivals that end in spectacular canoe races.

Nigerians have always maintained close links with the many rivers, large and small, that flow through their country. These rivers provide the people with a good supply of fish.

They also irrigate the land for growing crops. In some parts of the country the rivers are still the easiest way to travel. People use canoes to make trips or even to go to school, or to buy food.

The rivers are so important that some people think of them as gods and goddesses.

Regattas, or boat races, began as a way of giving thanks to these deities. Most riverside settlements hold regattas, but the

A model canoe shows people taking food to the market. At the regatta musicians play traditional instruments like the calabash.

most famous one is at Pategi, on the Niger.

The regatta is held near the river. There are dances representing many kinds of water creatures. People take a picnic to watch displays by swimmers and acrobats.

The highlight is a rowing race in brightly painted canoes. Strong rowers paddle the boats. Winning is not as important as taking part in an event that is enjoyed by everyone.

The most common form of jewelry in Nigeria is long strings of beads that people wear for special occasions like the regatta. As they have been for hundreds of years, the beads are made of polished glass and brightly colored stones.

OSUN CEREMONY

Every year the Yoruba people of southwest Nigeria worship the goddess of their local river with rituals, music, and sacrifices.

The old legends tell the story that the rivers were not always there. The rivers were once women. They were changed into rivers by the gods. The Osun River was a goddess. On the last Friday of August the Yoruba people worship her. The rituals take place around three shrines in Oshogbo, a town in the Yoruba country.

Rituals are led by the Ataoja, the ruler of Oshogbo. The Ataoja offers sacrifices to other gods of the area to ask them help to win the blessings of Osun. Drummers and singers follow him as he parades through the town's streets.

The king also gives gifts to his people. He holds a feast for the rich people and gives presents to all his poor subjects. These celebrations last for seven days. They go on throughout the night. On the eighth day the main ritual takes place on the

Kola nuts are offered to the river goddess. They are an important crop to the local people. The bronze warrior is from Benin, the Yorubas' old kingdom. Similar figures are placed near shrines.

banks of the river. A young priestess, called the Arugba, is led forward. She is painted all over, and must hold two kola nuts, uneaten, in her mouth for the whole day. In a trance, she leads a procession to the river, where the Ataoja feeds the river fish to please the Osun.

The women crowd around the river. They ring bells, pray to the goddess, and drink river water. The Osun festival ends in great rejoicing.

Chickens are among the sacrifices made to Osun. Worshipers believe that the goddess likes good things to eat. The more valuable the animal, the more pleased she will be to receive it.

THE RIVER GODDESS

There are many stories of Osun, the river goddess.

They are also found in Brazil, taken there by Yorubas.

The stories explain our need for rain and rivers,

and how all life depends on a supply of water.

THIS IS THE STORY of Laro, a king who lived many years ago. He ruled over Osogbo, a village surrounded by farms and country folk, and built near the banks of the mighty Osun River.

Everyone in Osogbo depended on this river. They drove their animals down to the river to drink, and during the dry season they carried its water back to their parched fields. They built boats to row swiftly and to go fishing.

One year the rains did not come when they were supposed to. There was no rain for months. There was no longer a river, but a muddy stream. The crops dried up in the fields, and the farm animals and the wild ones started dying.

People were hungry and frightened.

King Laro consulted the elders. The old men reminded him that the Osun was more than a river. Long ago the river had been a human woman, but she had turned into water and become a goddess. Osun was clearly upset with King Laro and his people. But the king did not know why, and neither did his people. The animals gazed at him.

Very early one morning Laro climbed down to the empty riverbed and called out, "Osun, why are you punishing my people and all the animals?"

The king waited and waited until he was hot and very thirsty. He bowed his head on the dry riverbed. Suddenly

King Laro heard a soft voice, a voice like the tiny waves of the mighty Osun.

"You and your village have only ever taken from me," said the voice. "You never give anything back. You must sacrifice the farm animals to me. Give my fish your last supplies of yam and plantain and fufu flour."

"We have almost nothing left," the king whispered sadly. "We will die."

"You must give me everything you have," replied the wavelike voice, "and I will take care of you and the beasts."

Laro nodded his head in obedience. He waited for more, but there were no voices, no sounds, only the sun and the silent animals lying in the shade.

The next day King Laro sacrificed the last three animals in the village – a goat and two chickens. He lifted the gourds and shook the last of the grain onto the dry riverbed. As he finished, the sky turned dark with a huge rain cloud. Water fell from the sky.

Although the rain did not stop for three days, the animals galloped with joy; the people leapt into their boats and fished in the river. They ran to their fields to start planting. Osun kept her promise. She would look after them if they cared for her. And every year since, on the same day the people of Osogbo have brought their sacrifices and grain to the river.

SALLAH

The Islamic fast called Ramadan takes place at different times each year. Nigeria's Muslims celebrate the end of the 30-day fast with Sallah.

This stringed instrument is a little like a guitar, with a hollow box that amplifies the vibrations made by the five strings.

Muslims are supposed to fast in *Ramadan*, the ninth month of the Muslim year. They are not allowed to eat or drink between sunrise and sunset. At the end of the long fast everyone has a grand celebration.

The main Sallah celebrations take place in northern Nigeria, where most Muslims live. The most elaborate festival is in the town of Katsina. Here, thousands gather for the main event. This is the *Durbar*, a colorful procession of horsemen in bright, ornate costumes. Durbar is an old Persian word that means house or court.

The first Durbars were held when the British used to rule Nigeria. The British ruler, who was called the *viceroy*, held magnificent ceremonies to show the Nigerians that the British were in charge. After the British left Nigeria, the Nigerians still held the Durbar. There are

Muslim ruler, called the *Emir*. He rides in the middle of the parade. Before him come horsemen of the Hausa-Fulani people. They wear coats of armor, scarlet turbans, and copper helmets topped with plumes of feathers. The horses have decorated manes and tails, and brightly colored bridles.

Then comes the Emir, in robes of white and carrying a parasol embroidered with silver. After the Emir are his guards, then wrestlers flexing their muscles. The crowd dances and sings to the musicians playing their drums, lutes, and fiddles.

For the Sallah everyone puts on clothes made of bright cloth like this. The warriors carry heavily decorated weapons.

people who think that it belongs to the past and has no place in Nigeria now that it is independent.

The focus of the Durbar is the local

HOW TO MAKE A FAN

*These fans are identical copies of Nigerian designs,
but ours are made from materials to be found at
home and not of leather and ostrich feathers.*

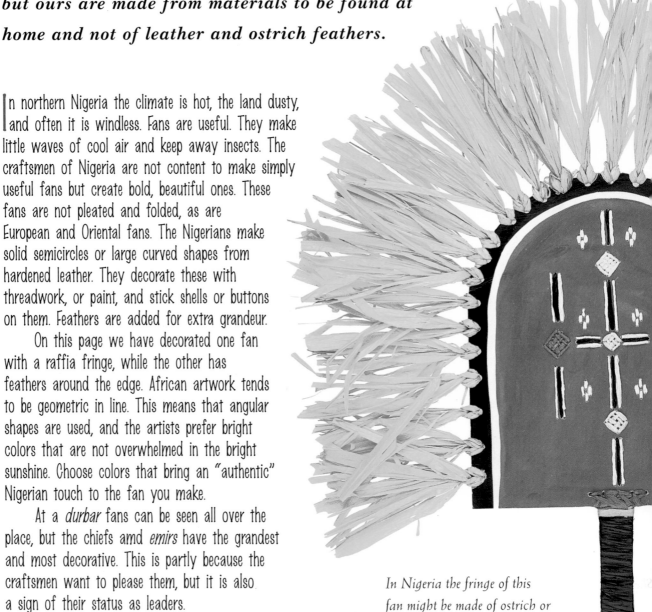

In northern Nigeria the climate is hot, the land dusty, and often it is windless. Fans are useful. They make little waves of cool air and keep away insects. The craftsmen of Nigeria are not content to make simply useful fans but create bold, beautiful ones. These fans are not pleated and folded, as are European and Oriental fans. The Nigerians make solid semicircles or large curved shapes from hardened leather. They decorate these with threadwork, or paint, and stick shells or buttons on them. Feathers are added for extra grandeur.

On this page we have decorated one fan with a raffia fringe, while the other has feathers around the edge. African artwork tends to be geometric in line. This means that angular shapes are used, and the artists prefer bright colors that are not overwhelmed in the bright sunshine. Choose colors that bring an "authentic" Nigerian touch to the fan you make.

At a *durbar* fans can be seen all over the place, but the chiefs amd *emirs* have the grandest and most decorative. This is partly because the craftsmen want to please them, but it is also a sign of their status as leaders.

*In Nigeria the fringe of this
fan might be made of ostrich or
eagle feathers. We used raffia.*

1 Take a piece of cardboard about 24 inches long and 8 inches wide. Fold it in half. Cut the open corners, two at a time, so that they curve to form an arch shape. Cover one of the surfaces with paint, and wait for it to dry. This will be the front of your fan. Now unfold the cardboard, and cut a 2-inch-wide slit in the center of the fold.

2 Draw a design on the reverse of the fan's painted side. Take a craft needle, and make holes at regular intervals along the lines of your design. Now thread the lengths of raffia or yarn through the holes, making a pattern on the painted side. Tape the feathers to the inside edges of the cardboard.

3 Cut out two pieces of cardboard, each about 6 inches long and 2 inches wide, and tape them together into a T-shape. Slide the trunk of the "T" through the slit to make a handle. Wrap raffia or yarn around it until it feels comfortable to hold. Stick the two sides of the fan together with glue. Finally, stitch the top of the "T" to the fan with raffia or yarn.

YOU WILL NEED
Sheets of cardboard or a cardboard box
Strips of raffia or yarn
Feathers
A craft needle, some glue, and some tape
Poster paints

27

CHRISTMAS

Christmas is the most important festival of the year for more than 30 million Nigerian Christians.

Palm branches hung with Christmas balls decorate the homes of most Nigerians. Only the rich can afford pine or plastic trees.

Christmas in Nigeria is very like Christmas festivities held elsewhere. In the 19th century many Christian missionaries came to Nigeria from Europe. They brought their European Christmas traditions with them. Santa Claus comes on Christmas Eve, and presents are opened on Christmas morning, just as in many parts of Europe and America.

A few Christmas traditions in Nigeria are different, however. There are no pine trees in Nigeria, so most families decorate a palm tree instead. Wealthy people buy pine trees imported from Europe.

Chicken is usually the Christmas meal. Meat is expensive in Nigeria, so for many it is a great festive treat.

JOLLOFF CHICKEN

SERVES 4 TO 6

3 tomatoes
3 onions
Vegetable oil for frying
1 pound chicken pieces, skin removed
3 red bell peppers, cored, seeded, and chopped
1½ cups long-grain rice
Chicken stock
Salt and pepper

1 Slice 1 tomato and chop 2. Slice 1 onion and chop 2.
2 Heat 2 tbsp oil in large skillet. Fry onion slices for 5 minutes until golden. Add tomato slices, and fry 1 minute; leave aside.
3 Add 2 tbsp oil to pan. Fry chicken until golden on both sides. Remove from pan.
4 Put chopped tomatoes, onions, and peppers in pan. Fry until soft. Stir in rice. Put chicken on top. Add chicken stock to cover.

5 Bring to boil. Cover and simmer 30 minutes. Stir in onion and tomato slices, and heat through. Add salt and pepper to taste.

This nativity scene combines the familiar figures and animals with simple Nigerian carving and colors.

29

INDEPENDENCE DAY

For centuries Nigeria fell to different rulers. The Benin empire rose and faded; sultans held sway. The British took power. But now Nigerians control their own country.

Nigeria became independent from British rule on October 1, 1960. The country had been a British colony for 60 years. It was one of the first African colonies in the British Empire to gain self-rule. Each year the Nigerians remember the proud day when they took charge of their own country.

The early years of independence were not easy in Nigeria. Civil war split the land as rival groups fought and tried to get power. A million Nigerians died.

Today October 1 is a day for everybody to celebrate what they have in common with each other, rather than the differences they feel between them.

Independence Day is a holiday for all the people. Some will go to grand balls, some to street parties or family dinners, as all Nigerians rejoice in the achievements of their nation.

On Independence Day the streets are full of people. Many are dressed in beautifully embroidered clothes or fabrics carrying symbols of their country and images of heroes and leaders.

Words to Know

Animism: The belief that things in nature, such as rivers and trees, possess spirits and, sometimes, supernatural powers.

Calabash: A hollow gourd used as a container or made into a musical instrument.

Deity: A god or goddess.

Emblem: A picture that stands for an idea.

Emir: The title given to a Muslim ruler. A Nigerian tribal chieftain.

Fast: To go without food deliberately.

Fufu flour: A basic food in African diets. It is made from ground roots (such as yams) and grains.

Gourd: A large fruit, similar to a squash, that has a very hard skin. When scooped out and dried, gourds make excellent containers.

Irrigate: To supply the land with water.

Pavilion: A decorative building that is used for entertainment or sports.

Pidgin: A simplified language that contains words from two or more languages. A pidgin language helps people who do not share a common language to communicate. In time, a pidgin can become a complicated language on its own.

Plantain: Bananalike fruit that is eaten cooked.

Regatta: A sports event featuring boat races.

Ritual: A religious ceremony that must be performed in a certain way or order.

Sallah: In Nigeria the celebration that marks the end of the Islamic fast period of Ramadan.

Totem: An admired animal or object from nature that a tribal person or group chooses as its emblem.

Trance: A mysterious, sleeplike state that is difficult to wake from.

ACKNOWLEDGMENTS

WITH THANKS TO:

Africa Centre, London fly whisk p8, drum, dolls p14, wooden animals, musical instruments p20-24. Anthony Adeloye p30. Nigerian High Commission, London mask, cross p6-7, gourd p8, mask p14, brass figure p21. Vale Antiques, Elgin Avenue, London brass figure p12.

PHOTOGRAPHS BY:

All photographs by Bruce Mackie. Cover photograph by ZEFA.

ILLUSTRATIONS BY:

Alison Fleming title page, Robert Shadbolt p4-5, Mountain High Maps ® Copyright © 1993 Digital Wisdom, Inc. p4-5. Philip Divine p7. Philip Bannister p11. Norman Bancroft-Hunt p22-23.

SET CONTENTS